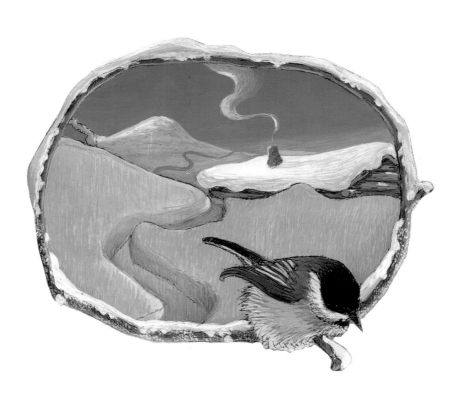

Otava Book Printing Ltd
Keuruu 1999

ISBN 951-1-16392-2

Pekka Vuori

KORVATUNTURI

Tales from Land of Santa Claus

written and illustrated by Pekka Vuori
translated from the Finnish by Tim Steffa

Otava Publishing Co. Ltd.
Helsinki

The brush, the eye and Korvatunturi fjeld

Not all that long ago, about a century back, Santa Claus summoned all the master elves to an important meeting. Zip, the chief postal elf, displayed a heap of letters as tall as a reindeer calf. They all contained inquiries about Santa's grandfather clock, the growth of the elves' beards, the pattern of Mrs. Claus' bonnet, the running speed of reindeer, and other subjects regarding life here in the realm of stocking caps. Some writers asked what a smoke sauna was, others wanted to climb the big lookout tower. As curious visitors would have interfered with Korvatunturi activities, it was decided to print an illustrated narrative for those interested. All eyes turned to me, chief of the artist elves, old Scumble. By general acclamation, I was given the responsibility for creating this book. The printing, of course, was entrusted to the Korvatunturi book and postcard press; I have painted a picture of it on page 31. Cooperation with the printing-press elves went so well that the book was ready well in advance of the year 2000, when Santa Claus turns 1500 years of age.

Scumble

*Chief of the artist elves
since the year 1648*

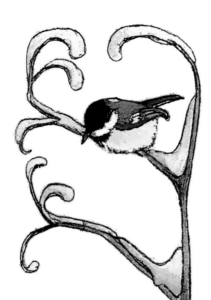

Welcoming in the New Year with a song

It must be admitted that after the Christmas rush we sleep late at Korvatunturi. Santa's house lies silent beneath a thick blanket of snow. Somewhere nearby a bear also sleeps deep, hibernating in its den. But it's not long before fires are kindled in the stoves and paths tramped through the snow. More firewood is sawn in the woodshed, and bright elfin song sounds from the laundry. For a moment golden sunbeams break over the peaks of the fjelds. The days gradually begin to lengthen. Santa Claus brings out his ledger. Once again it's time to begin thinking about Christmas.

Mrs. Claus hums though Santa's stomach rumbles

Mrs. Claus is well aware that wild frozen cranberries are Santa's favorite breakfast treat. Colander, the kitchen elf, grins sleepily, having been·asked to fetch rye bread, jam and reindeer cheese.

Tame bullfinches make themselves at home indoors, carefully scouring the table and floor for bread crumbs and other scraps of food. They are considerably plumper than those flitting about the nearby woods. Smudge, the household dog, has just had five whimpering pups. A bowl is filled with milk for her, and she in turn suckles the pups on canine milk. They're sure to grow in no time at all into fine reindeer-herders.

At home
high atop a stump

The folks of Elfenville are
awakened by the awful
squawking of a jay. This is
followed by a piercing screech
that rouses the inhabitants of
every cabin in the valley.
The jay is an even better alarm
clock than the elf Nudge,
whose job it is to get
sleepyheads out of bed
and working at their many tasks.
Smoke soon curls into the sky
as breakfast porridge simmers
on each and every wood stove.
Not all the elves make their
homes here in Elfenville.
Hundreds of red-capped
helpers also inhabit the yard
of Santa's huge house.
Mill elves thrive in nooks
and crannies among burlap
bags of grain; scores of sauna
elves live in the darkness of
the bathhouse. The miniature
elves, or gnomes, occupy a
niche all their own.

Korvatunturi, here we come!

An unexpected guest, Snicker, arrives for Santa's birthday party. The great grey owl, Hoot, has accompanied this curly-bearded gnome on his return to Lapland from France. The return trip took nearly ten years. Snicker's bag holds a birthday gift for Santa and a picture postcard of a huge tower under construction in Paris.

The party guests are amused at how Snicker has learned in France to speak through his nose.
Food is what interests the owl. 'What, nothing but reindeer cheese? And here I'm used to dining on well ripened camembert!'

'That's a touching song,' Santa said,
'straight from the heart
via the beard.'

An unexpected gift in 1900
to 1400-year-old Santa Claus:
a newfangled pocket watch,
direct from Paris.

The postponed birthday celebrations

Everyone on Korvatunturi fjeld knows that Santa Claus was born on Christmas Eve. But the busy season leaves no time for celebration.

So it's always shifted toward New Year's Day. Everyone drinks mead and bilberry juice, and eats cinnamon rolls and flaky honey pastries. There's dancing in the huge main room (on the table as well). Toward evening the sauna elves give Santa a bath, washing him with tar soap and massaging him with juniper oil. Santa and Mrs. Claus have the birthday meal at the long table with the master elves. They're served mushroom pies and fish soup seasoned with herbs. The evening concludes with a performance by the Korvatunturi Theater of 'The Mill Elf's Baggy Pants.'

The vanishing
concert hall

The gnomes first build a charming
miniature snow castle. Then other elves
begin to add more rooms and towers.
Eventually all the Korvatunturi elves
join together in the work. They create a
white Winter Palace. It is hollowed out to
make a Music Chamber for use by the elfin
choir and orchestra. A giant snowman
goes up beside it. In spring this entire
spectacle melts. In summer pale, delicate
wintergreen blossoms where it once stood.
Everyone agrees to build an even better
snow castle next winter.

The little boy who liked jam

Somewhere far away, in a remote corner of Lapland, there towers a huge stone pillar, the Axle of the World. Santa's cabin once stood at the foot of this pillar, but it vanished centuries ago. At least once every ten years Santa Claus makes a solitary pilgrimage to the landscape of the Axle of the World. He strolls around, listening to the birds and savoring his lunch. In a cupboard back home at Korvatunturi fjeld he still has a few artefacts of his childhood: a slightly charred drawing of a boy gobbling some jam, a faded rag doll, a cracked chamber pot. He has some linen pants with a flap and a little sled that was also used as a cradle. When Santa was only a baby he'd often been rocked in it . . .

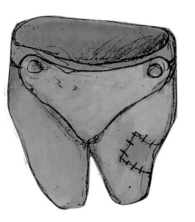

Fit rockers to a sled, and it turns into a cradle.

The greybeards of Christmas Valley

Not all old elves are master elves, but all master elves are very old, though still not as old as Santa Claus. They are resourceful, grey-bearded old scallywags. As a rule the master elves, supervised by Santa, convene each Friday at the long plank table for mutual deliberation. Elfin scribes record decisions in the birchbark-bound *Chronicle of the Greybeards*.

Fife is director of the elfin orchestra and choir. His main interest is all kinds of wind instruments, such as birchbark horns, reed and willow panpipes. The gnomes performing with the orchestra play faintly-sounding grass flutes. To supplement the elfin choir, Fife has recruited a few tame starlings.

Master elf Jot and his helpers plan most of the Korvatunturi buildings and are always on hand with their measures to oversee the work of the joinery elves. Jot is particularly keen on designing wooden toys. Jot takes on as apprentices any young elves who hope to become joiners.

Scrub is in charge of cleaning, the laundry and other housekeeping affairs. The stocking-capped cleaning corps, with its brooms, soap and dust mops, makes short work of the tasks assigned by Scrub. In other words, he sees to it that Mr. and Mrs. Claus always have clean pyjamas available.

Headmaster Jaunt's button-eyed, red-capped pupils don't sit at desks in a classroom, they tramp around the woods or go boating on the river. Jaunt teaches about plants and animals – from aardvarks to zinnias – out in the wilds. Pupils might study the elfin primer while perched on a lofty limb. (Their primer may be seen on page 31.)

Glyph the writer elf always has pen, writing pad and ink bottle at hand. As the bard of Korvatunturi, he sharpens his quill the instant a birthday requires a poem of tribute or the Korvatunturi Theater happens to need a fresh, action-packed play for its repertoire.

Here is Glyph's poem, 'A Sauna Elf Goes to the Circus':

For Suds the sauna elf
stripes are quite a passion.
As he has said himself:
'They're the height of fashion.'
At the circus the elfin band
gave the zebra a great big hand.
But Suds just winced and cried:
'That horse's stripes are phoney!'
To this the rest replied:
'They are real all right,
but you are full of baloney!'

Theater director Hokum pulls laughter right out of his hat. The fact is, he's an accomplished liar – on stage, that is. He's noticed that an audience has fun when someone babbles outright balderdash from the footlights. He's a short elf specializing in tall tales.

At five in the morning a spruce topples

It's a peaceful winter's evening. Big snowflakes fall silently, blanketing Elf Valley in soft snow. But at midnight the wind rises, howling in corners. The great trees groan and the surrounding forest roars. The light sleepers wake first and before long Santa is also up, amazed by the force of the gale. Trees are blowing over: there's no going out tonight.

By morning the storm has passed. Master Jot
goes out to inspect the damage. A spruce has toppled,
caving in the workshop roof. Though the Elfenville cabins
and sheds have also suffered, it's the worst of the damage.
Within three days everything is
repaired and Santa is able
to smile again.

The deft hands and practised eyes of the joinery elves

Joinery elves are not merely cabinetmakers, they are also accomplished sculptors. They are often at their benches until the wee hours. This is especially true before the spring woodworking show and the competition for the rank of Master Joiner of the Year. Korvatunturi's huge wood warehouse holds great stacks of ancient planks. All the same, squabbles break out there as each of the joinery elves tries to saw for himself the choicest lengths of knotless wood. But when master elf Jot appears on the scene, all bickering ends at once and the only sound is that of furious sawing.

*A drinking cup with a handle,
hollowed out of walnut.*

*An easy chair of pine
decorated with bear heads.*

Santa's coat of arms,
carved of alder.
The escutcheon
is in red and gold.

Shellac,
Master Joiner of 1900,
with his sculpture
'The Great
Guardian Elf.'

A large
fish scoop
carved from
birch.

29

The call of the red, peaked cap

Here we see the Korvatunturi press,
which is some four hundred years old.
Its portly foreman, Chubby, also a master elf,
carefully inspects each printed page.
He mastered the secrets of paper-making
and printing as a young elf in Germany.
He has more than enough faithful helpers,
for the red, peaked cap of the printer is held in
high esteem. Some of the printer elves are color mixers,
others make paper from old rags, still others
have learned the art of bookbinding.
But only Chubby knows how to make
the plates required for printing.
The elfin primer is the oldest product of the press.
Aided by this book, unlettered elfin children
have learned to read and write the alphabet,
supervised by headmaster Jaunt.
He won't accept just any old scrawl.

THE ELFIN PRIMER	A	B	C	D	E

 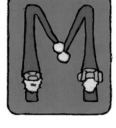  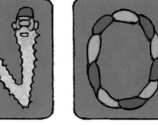  

     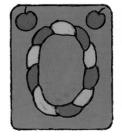

A strange star falls in the night

One evening Doodle, one of the most experienced of draftsman elves, is awake in his tower chamber. He is inspecting a remarkable new device: a photographic box which instantly produces perfectly genuine looking pictures. Even the quickest draftsman is no match for it. He glances out the round window at the sky: a bright, glittering star appears to be streaking across the heavens straight toward Korvatunturi fjeld! A long whistling sounds, then a whiz and a thump. He must hurry and tell Santa at once. Early next morning Doodle finds a smoking crater, clearly made by a meteor. He takes a picture of it and then does his best to calm some frightened Siberian jays. Santa and his wife arrive on the spot and soon the other folk of Elf Valley gather to wonder at the blackened pit. 'A close call!' they all exclaim in chorus.

An elf beats Santa at his own game

Chess is a favorite pastime at Korvatunturi fjeld. The checkered board looks familiar, but the pieces are rather strange. The King is Santa Claus, the Queen his wife. The Knight is a rampant reindeer, the Castle a stone granary, and the Bishop a thin courier elf.

And what of the Pawns? Their place is occupied, of course, by gnomes. Tub, the wisest of the sauna elves, uses tactics in his game. He's always coming up with sudden, unexpected moves.

They leave his opponents baffled. Santa has been playing chess for hundreds of years. He is a highly experienced but cautious player. After a sauna, he and Tub often sit beard to beard at the chessboard. We elves gather around to watch them. 'Tub's checked him with a reindeer!' Where to go from here? Santa Claus is perplexed. Yet another surprise from Tub?

Mrs. Claus Santa A Courier

A Reindeer A Granary A Gnome

Spring comes, Gold River thaws

Though thick drifts have piled up over winter,
spring finally comes to Korvatunturi fjeld as well.
The days lengthen and the ice leaves Gold River.
Frank the postman elf pauses on the arched bridge
to watch as three smews fly overhead.
A swan struts the rim of the ice in search of a mate.
Frank feels they're all sure signs of spring.
Spring also brings gold fever to Korvatunturi.
Once the river waters have warmed a little,
dozens of eager gold-panners appear on the banks.
Swirling their huge pans, they tenaciously sift
the riverbank sands for gold. All elves carry leather
pouches at their belts. These may be bulging with
gold when the elves come home. This is melted
down and minted into tiny gold pieces.
These Korvatunturi coins are used to purchase
all sorts of necessities from the south.

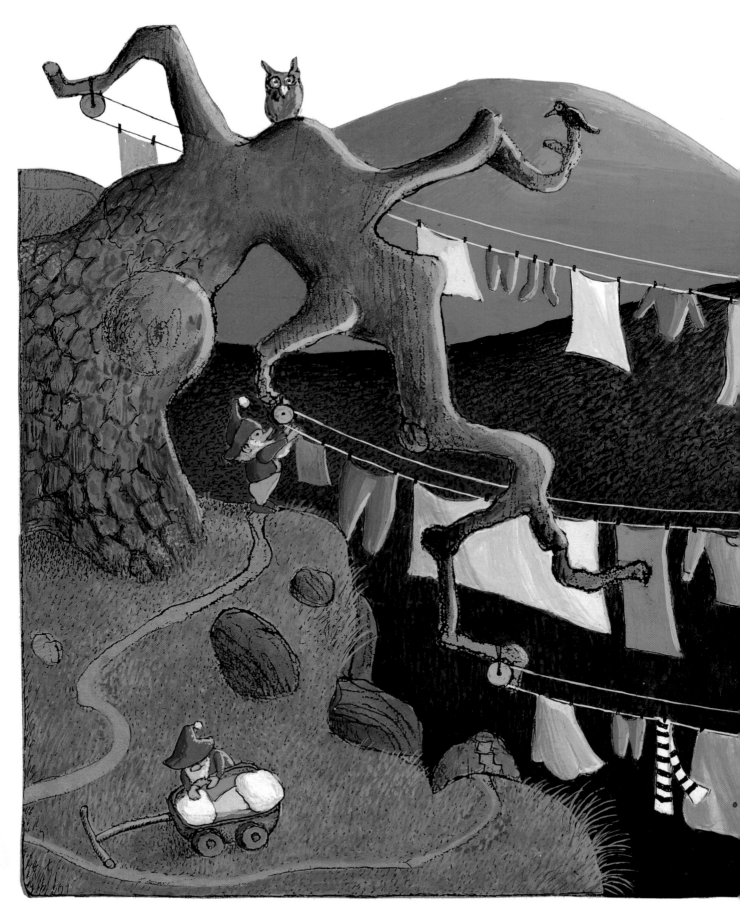

There's no fear of laundry day here

See for yourself: laundry abounds at Korvatunturi.
That calls for a lot of clean water and pine soap.
Laundry day means a splendid flag display: all sorts
of clothing hangs from the lines, from gnome trousers to
Mrs. Claus' underskirts. The laundry owl is perched
at its post in a tall pine, making sure that songbirds don't
alight on the lines and soil the clean laundry.

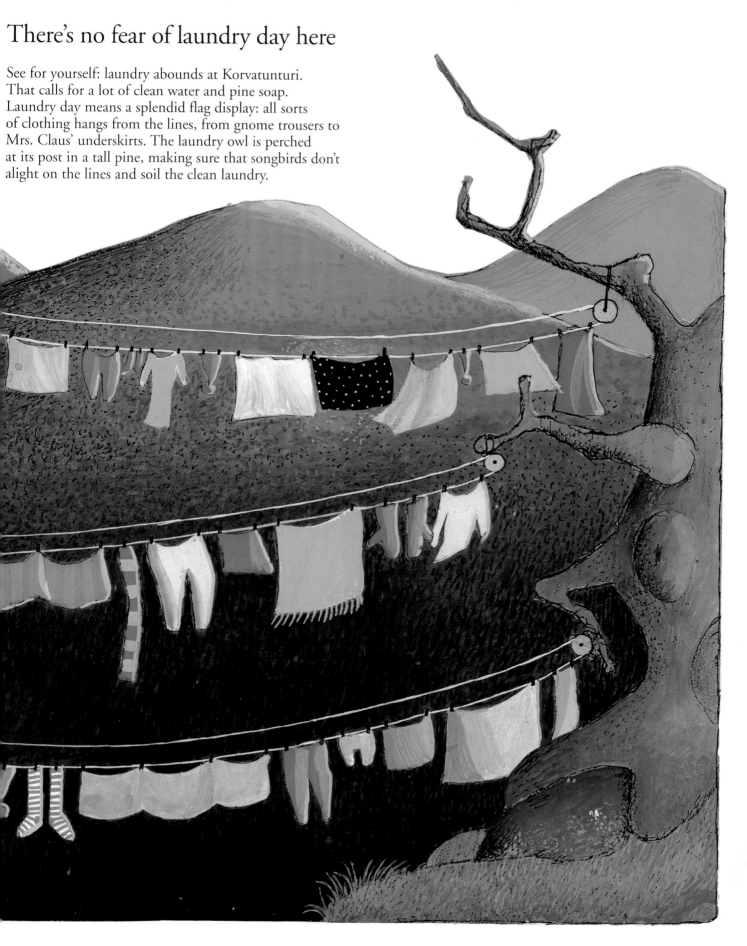

A summer island: the perfect place for a holiday

Every year in June Santa Claus
leaves Lapland and Korvatunturi
to his elves. He sets off on his summer
holiday in the south, in central Finland.
Santa, his wife, and their elfin aides
travel in reindeer-drawn carts.
Such a procession is rarely seen farther
south. On the island of Sumiainen
there await Santa a log cabin, a sauna,
a fishing pole, sauna steam and a swim
in the lake. He's dreamed of all this
through the months of winter cold.
On the very first evening, he sits
on a lakeside rock and fishes for perch.
From the cabin, the delicious
aroma of cooking greets his nose:
Mrs. Claus is making pancakes.

Who's afraid of an old sauna elf?

Korvatunturi's huge smoke sauna
is a pitch-dark as a bogeyman's cave.
Its log walls are black with soot
and redolent of birch leaves.
There are many other saunas at Korvatunturi,
but this is the biggest and oldest of them all.
Whisk, the oldest of the sauna elves,
knows it must be heated with alder
and the water carried from the spring.
There is no whistling or quarreling in a sauna.
This the elfin children learn at an early age.
Sometimes, though, quite a water fight
can break out on the sauna benches.
When this happens, Whisk,
the old geezer in the striped
shirt, orders everyone
out to a birch grove
to learn how to make
birch-twig whisks.

The island
of lazy elves

Reindeer Brook flows serenely
just beyond Korvatunturi fjeld.
It takes curious twists and turns
along the way, but finally ends
in little Heart Pond.

Elf Island, round and verdant,
is right in its center. You get there
by crossing an arched wooden bridge,
by rowboat, by swimming, or even
by swimming there underwater,
as some sauna elves do. On the island
the elfin folk loll around, playing,
doing crafts, or dozing. There is a
jointly built log cabin, storehouse,

boat shed, and a sod-covered sauna.
The island is at its best in summer:
you can sail, row, fish,
and swim around the island.
In winter a hole is cut in the ice.
Without batting an eye, the elves
plunge into the icy water
and then streak, bright red,
to the sauna to warm up again.

Berry-picking with a bear

In autumn, food must be stored in Korvatunturi's
cellars for winter. The elves become hamsters,
gathering everything from cabbages to cranberries.
It sometimes happens that rivals show up
simultaneously at a berry-picking site.
The elves know that the marshes abound
with berries enough for bears and elves alike.
In autumn bears are usually fat and happy.
A boggy marsh is really no temptation.
So the elves can fill their baskets in peace and quiet.
Ravens provide advice on other berry-picking places.

The gnomes dwell beneath a spruce

No one knows exactly how many gnomes there are – not the master elves, not even Santa. Instead of living in Elfenville, they have built their own little houses out of sight, beneath trees trunks, in rocky crevices, in the saunas, or beneath the floors of the storage sheds. Their small size is a big advantage. The cleaning of a low oven or cramped room is best seen to by gnomes. They are Korvatunturi's best mushroom authorities and pickers. They instantly recognize a good, non-poisonous, edible mushroom, check underneath to see if its wormy, and then fell it with their little saws. The mushrooms must be cut up at once, for not even the smallest of chanterelles will fit into their tiny baskets.

Seven red caps

At a bend in Reindeer Brook, beyond the big woods, stands the house of seven elfin brothers. Their names, from oldest to youngest, are: Jonathan, Thomas, Arthur, Simeon, Timothy, Lawrence and Edward.
They are not Korvatunturi elves, they're Santa's nearest neighbors. The brothers' red, wood-shingled farm shows faintly in the distance from the peak of Korvatunturi fjeld. The elfin brothers are animal lovers and nature conservationists. They even understand the language of animals. They can sometimes be heard conversing with the great grey shrikes flitting about the farmyard. On long woodland treks, they rest beneath a lean-to warmed by a blazing fire.

51

The folks of Korvatunturi put their faith in the great grandfather clock and the almanac

The first snowfall brings to mind winter and the coming Christmas. Santa's grandfather clock is set to chime as early as six o'clock in the morning. It sometimes happens that Santa oversleeps. If nothing is seen or heard from him, Mrs. Claus dispatches one of the kitchen elves to tickle Santa's feet. It's a sure means of waking him. Master Cog keeps the old clock in running order. He has three technical gnomes as helpers and they're just the size to go scrambling about the clockworks. They make repair and maintenance a breeze. Cog has learned to know the cycles of the moon and stars. Each year he composes an almanac for the denizens of Korvatunturi. It records the daily round and includes the elves' and reindeers' birthdays.

Postmaster Zip

Mail delivery posthaste

It's Postmaster Zip who
determines the movement of
the mail at Korvatunturi.
Throughout the autumn the
mailbags grow fatter and fatter.
Transporting them requires
stout draft reindeer, huge
sledges and sleighs, and
many a strapping elf.
Though mail delivery
often calls for speed,
the postal elves sometimes
get carried away.
Barrelling down the fjeld
slopes, the reindeer and
sleighs seem to take to the air.
Hoot the owl, fresh back from
France, observes it all wide-eyed.
He's never seen the like,
not even in Paris traffic!
In the summertime the mail
moves with less dispatch
than over the winter snows,
the letters travelling at walking
speed either by pack reindeer
or in birch-bark rucksacks
borne by elves. Larger
mailbags can also be
conveyed by rowboat
on Reindeer Brook.

Tons of wishes

As Christmas approaches, Santa seems almost overwhelmed by a high stack of letters. Although he reads children's letters late into the night, most of the correspondence must be left to the scribe elves. Hauling the heavy mailbags around calls for considerable reindeer-power. That's why the reindeer are not required to do it several years in a row. Rudolf, Korvatunturi's most famous reindeer, was originally a post-office worker. He was then promoted to pulling Santa's sled on Christmas Eve. Rudolf is now retired. He observes daily life around the Korvatunturi precincts. Santa's plump bullfinches enjoy perching on Rudolf's antlers.

Let's get cooking

The huge bake oven is the heart of Korvatunturi's kitchen, and rosy-nosed Vittles its soul. Without the sprightly kitchen elves, cooking wouldn't really amount to much. Vittles hardly has time to express his desire for bread, and the elves are already busy rolling out the dough.
Mrs. Claus and her helpers tend to the pantries and cellars, Vittles to the preparation of meals. And the food at Korvatunturi?

The favorites, at least, are oven-baked barley porridge, fish soup, toasted reindeer cheese, perch in a pastry crust, rutabaga pies, grilled salmon, bilberry tarts, and pancakes with cloudberry jam. Spring water and reindeer milk are the drinks, along with mead on special occasions.

Pine-cone reindeer and wooden swings

Almost all the elfin families, those of the gnomes as well, include children. Elfin children are small, but those of gnomes are, to be sure, very tiny indeed. This means that at birth they can fit into a matchbox.

These Lilliputians sleep in sweet little hammocks woven of bast. Elfin children grow up quickly and before long they're already romping on the floor or playing ball or even somersaulting on the grass outdoors. On trips to the woods they collect pine cones, stones, or strangely gnarled branches.

From these they build pine-cone reindeer, twig huts, or stone towers and forts. In winter the slopes offer excellent sled runs, and the crystal-clear ice of the pond is an invitation to ice skating games. With the years, the tips of the elf boys' chins eventually sprout beards. The girls' hair grows until their plaits sometimes reach all the way to the ground.

60

Much snow, little to eat

It's an ordinary winter.
A lot of snow falls,
and the next day,
a lot more.
One more major blizzard,
and the drifts now exceed
anything in elfin memory.
Even the trees bend
beneath the weight of
the snow.
The squirrels, their hoards
of food hidden somewhere
beneath drifts where
they can't find them,
are going hungry.
Santa's neighbors,
the wise elfin brothers,
have noticed this.
They provide the
squirrels with pine cones
and acorns from their
winter stores.
Santa also dispatches
some Korvatunturi elves
to the food relief effort.
So the squirrels survive
this winter as well.

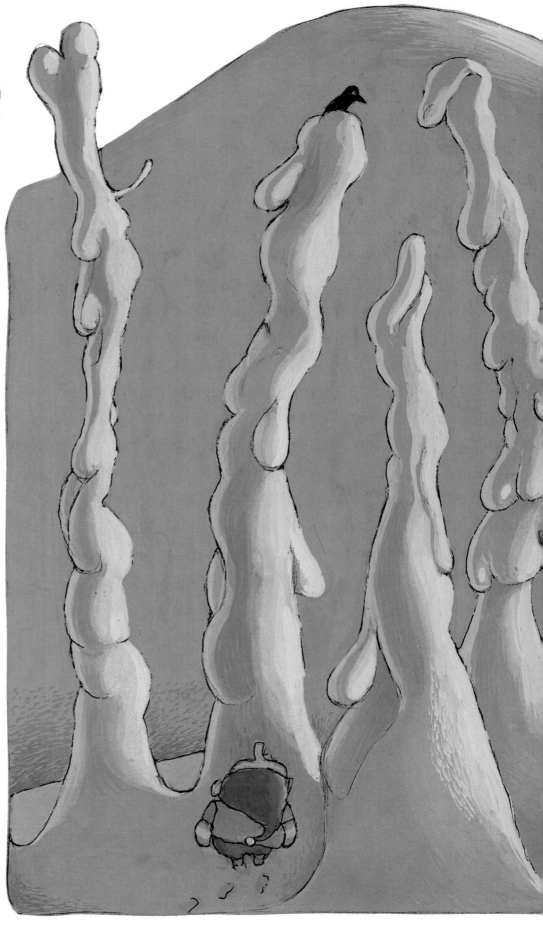

There's always time for admiring the northern lights

Beyond Korvatunturi fjeld stands
a look-out tower constructed of logs.
It is from there that master elf
Cog often observes curious
celestial events. He is fascinated
in particular by comets and the
northern lights. No one is able to
predict with any certainty when
the northern lights will begin to glow.
When they do, he must quickly
scramble up the tower
with his notebook and telescope.
In the old days it was believed
in Lapland that the northern lights
were the result of a giant fox
flicking its tail against the fjeld slopes.
The sparks this produced
gave rise to the heavenly 'foxfire.'
But master elf Cog knows
that the northern lights
are a peculiar electrical phenomenon.
This is why he carefully records
what he sees in his notebook.
The folks of Korvatunturi believe
that if you see a shooting star
and the northern lights at
the same time, it will bring
you luck.

A reindeer ride fits the bill

Without reindeer Korvatunturi wouldn't really be Korvatunturi. The elves learn as children how to get along perfectly with these antlered creatures: how to harness them, drive them and, of course, milk them. As Christmas approaches the draft reindeer, sledges and harness are seen to. By Christmas Eve everything must be in travelling condition. In summer or periods of scant snow, the draft reindeer handle transport, their flanks slung with panniers. Reindeer are fond of lichen, which they can even find beneath snow. They also eat various mushrooms whenever they are available. Reindeer cows provide milk, a delicious drink, especially when flavored with a pinch of sorrel. Reindeer milk is also made into a tasty white cheese. The round wheels of cheese are dried and stored in a cellar.

Korvatunturi's chief reindeer herder, master elf Trot, inspects drying cheeses.

The sun goes into hiding

As Christmas approaches, the sun shows less and less.
Blue twilight and darkness steal across Korvatunturi fjeld.
In the end the sun no longer rises above the horizon at all.
For the denizens of the tundra the only light is the moon, the stars
– and the candles that Master Scrub's helpers have been making and
storing in a shed since summer. This year something very annoying
happened: mice sneaked into the shed and nibbled hundreds
of candles, those of suet and wax alike, down to nubbins.
But this did provide the birds with an extra treat.

There's a little of the musician in every elf

In Headmaster Jot's school
elfin children learn to play instruments,
sing and beat drums. Fife chooses the
best of them as students in the choir
and orchestra. Elf Clef is Korvatunturi's
most popular composer. So catchy
are the melodies he conjures up on
his pump organ that even his dog
Dunce sings along, howling plaintively.
At midsummer the sun doesn't set
at Korvatunturi even in the middle
of the night. Everyone celebrates
the summer light then:
magic drums beat all night long,
everyone feasts and dances.
Santa can play the *kantele*.
When he brings out his five-stringed
instrument, everyone falls silent.
He alone still remembers the most
ancient of the Lapland lays.

Drama on both sides of the footlights

The plays by the Korvatunturi Theater are zany and extremely noisy. But the audience too laughs and yells so much that the actors can barely hear themselves. Their lines must be delivered in a shout, and the prompter gets completely befuddled. The current production is the play 'The Singing and Soaring Miss Wolf.' The lead actor is supposed to fly across the stage suspended on ropes. Suddenly the ropes break and the audience charges up on stage to assist the star after her forced landing.

The theater audience also understands corny jokes.

Making toys is no mean feat

Christmas is coming and from the workshop come sawing, metallic and banging sounds. An elfin army sews, planes, glues, paints and packs . . . The chief toy master, Bauble, has smudges of paint on his nose: that's how closely he inspects the freshly painted toys. Dolls, Teddy bears and sleds are always popular gifts, but the Drawing Office also invents fresh surprises such as steam engines and spinning monkeys. One gnome has fallen asleep in a gift box and ended up packed in a big bag of presents. The bag is already on a reindeer sled before a sharp squeal sounds, and the elf is rescued from becoming some child's gift.

Santa Claus heads for the woods

Having read thousands of letters and dictated just as many replies to an elfin scribe, Santa takes his well-tarred skis and juniper poles from a corner, and skis all the way out to Korvatunturi's broad hinterlands to inspect Christmas in the woods. Master Scrub and his corps of elves set candles out in the woods, the spruces are decorated as Christmas trees. The warm light attracts birds, squirrels, hares and many other animals, right down to harvest mice.

Even a timid wolverine braves the woods to wonder at this new phenomenon. Santa skis in silence through the vaulted, snowy forest. It's a good place to forget for a moment the workshop and the bulging mailbags.

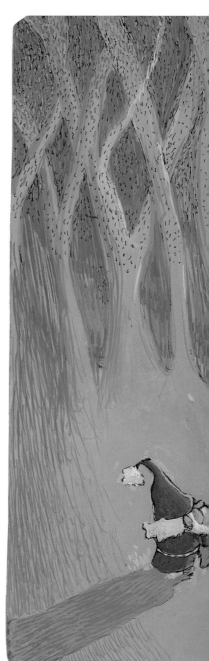

Santa's snack. Perch baked
in a rye crust keep hunger at bay.
The round lid is sliced off
with a sheath knife.

Santa's
walking stick.
It's carved from
a spruce root and
glossy, burnished
from centuries
of use.

Santa's flask.
A leather bottle
with a stopper of reindeer antler.
While travelling, Santa
usually drinks berry juice.

Taking out
the walking stick

A few days before Christmas
Santa and the master elves
gather yet again. There are
many issues to be considered
before Christmas Eve.
Are the gifts already packed?
Are the draft reindeer in
condition? What about the
addresses and routes?
They run through a long list.
The gifts going long distances
must be dispatched at once.
Santa takes his travelling garb
from the closet: his long,
red woollen cape and fur-
fringed cap. These he uses
only on Christmas Eve.
Mrs. Claus herself sewed
the sack for gifts in a colorful
patchwork. And then his
beard! He washes and combs
it, for the most important
day of the year will soon
be at hand.

Santa's travelling knife.
The decorated grip is carved of
reindeer antler.
The sheath is
woven of
birch bark.

Santa's compass.
The black frame
is inset with bone.

The long day, the happy night

In the morning twilight of Christmas Eve the draft reindeer and their sled are urged into motion. The fjelds are illuminated by only a faint glow from the clouds on the horizon. Santa double-checks on his compass the direction for each load of presents, since he himself does not have time to distribute all the gifts. There are occasional stops to eat and to feed the draft reindeer as well. As the trip continues, the pace simply increases. All seem to be floating over the silent valleys and frozen lakes. Santa's reindeer Blitzen is among the fleetest. The light of Christmas candles flickers in windows. Everyone awaits Santa's arrival. Sometimes the elves must use their lamps to find the correct street and house. But in the end all the gifts find their way into the right hands. As the night ends, Santa and his elves make their way home to Korvatunturi. Santa is now yearning for his own soft bed.

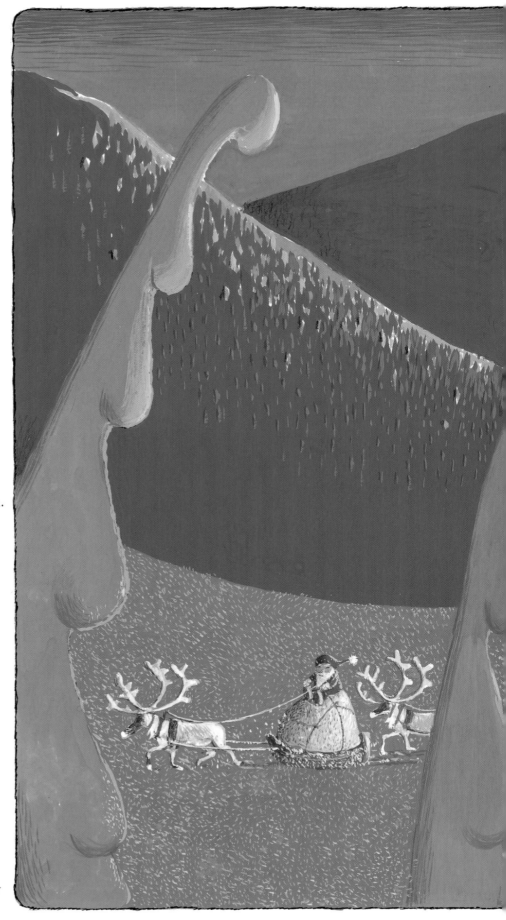

The travellers return hungry – and tired

Santa is home again, tucked in bed beneath his patchwork quilt. The draft reindeer are already asleep, but the wakeful driver elves still sit at the dining table, which master chef Vittles has set upon his return from the south. They're recalling the heap of snow that fell from a tree down the travellers' necks. Hokum, who has the longest of the elfin beards, recounts the strangest events of past decades. Sleep weighs heavy on everyone's eyes. Outside the temperature slowly falls. The trees and buildings stand mantled in snow beneath the starry sky. Soon everyone at Korvatunturi is fast asleep.